Japan Adventure
Coloring Book

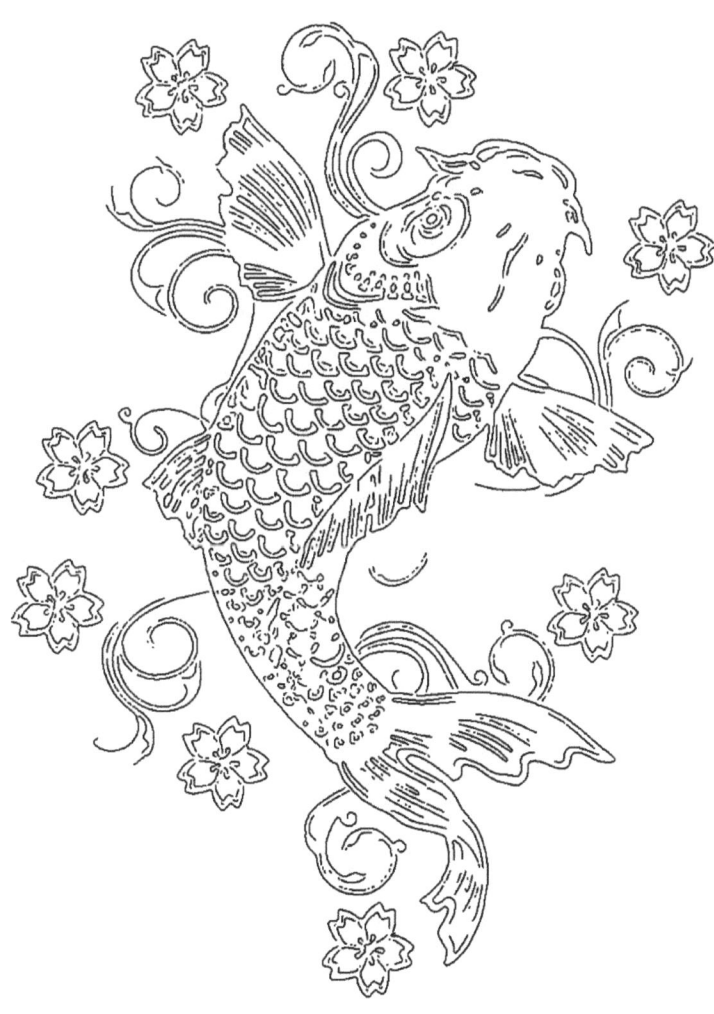

Marianne Garcia

Japan Adventure
Coloring Book

ISBN-13:978-1534779266

ISBN-10:1534779264

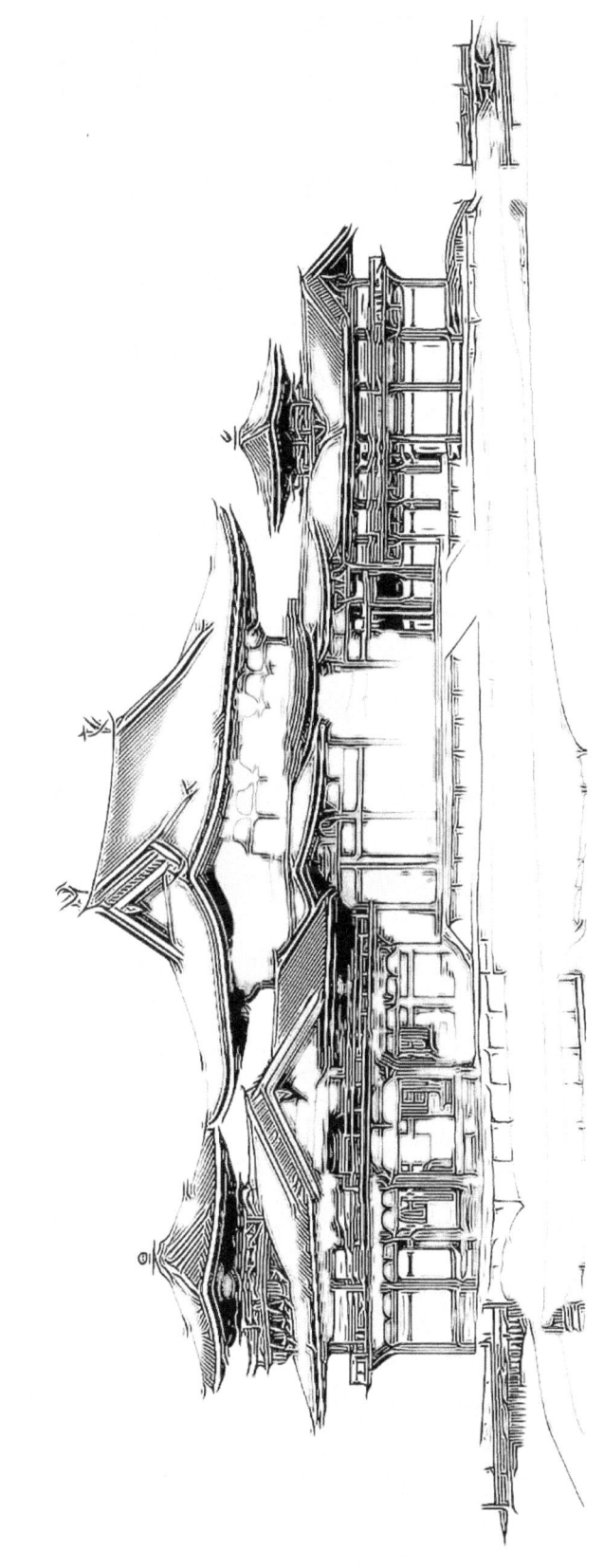

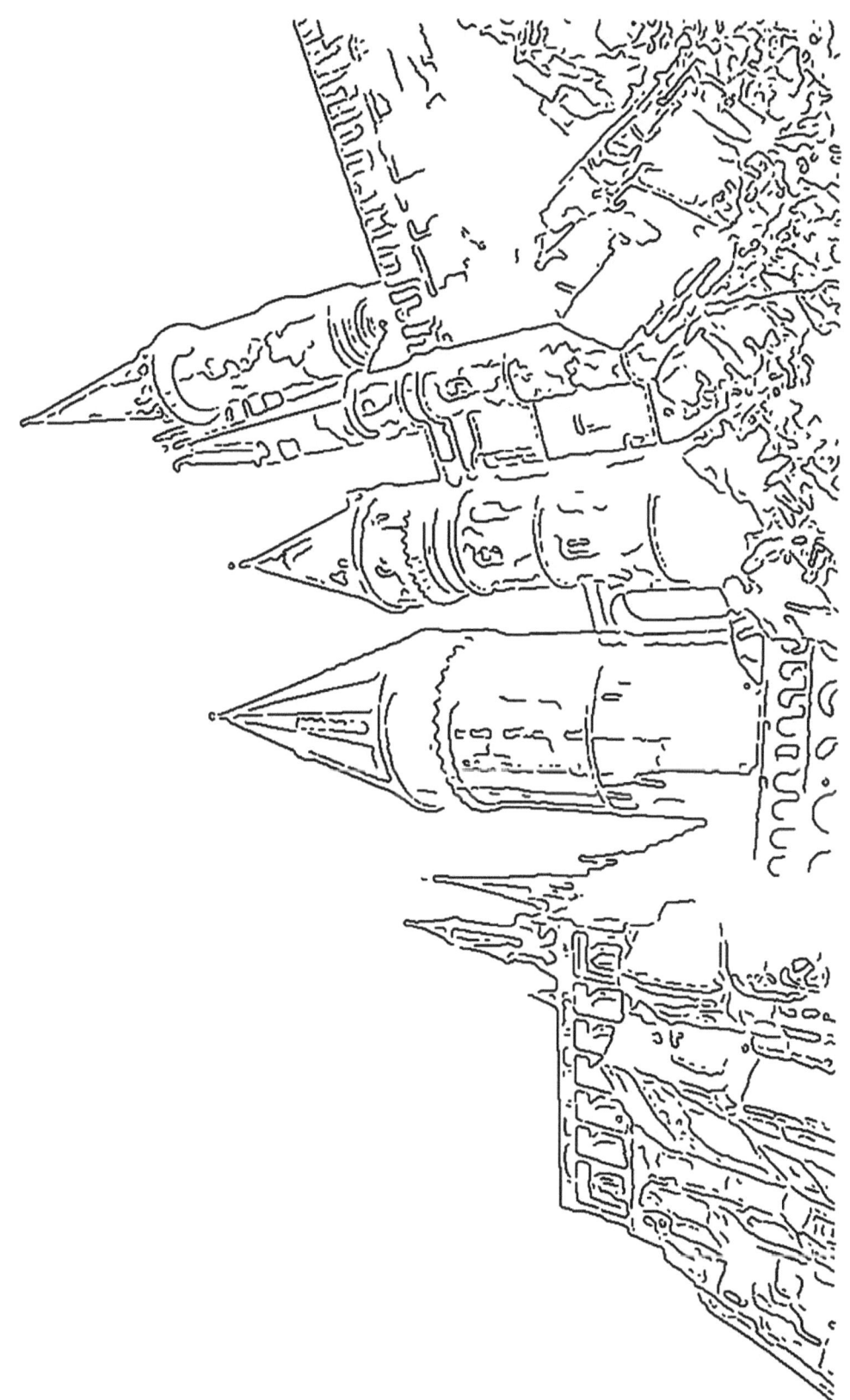

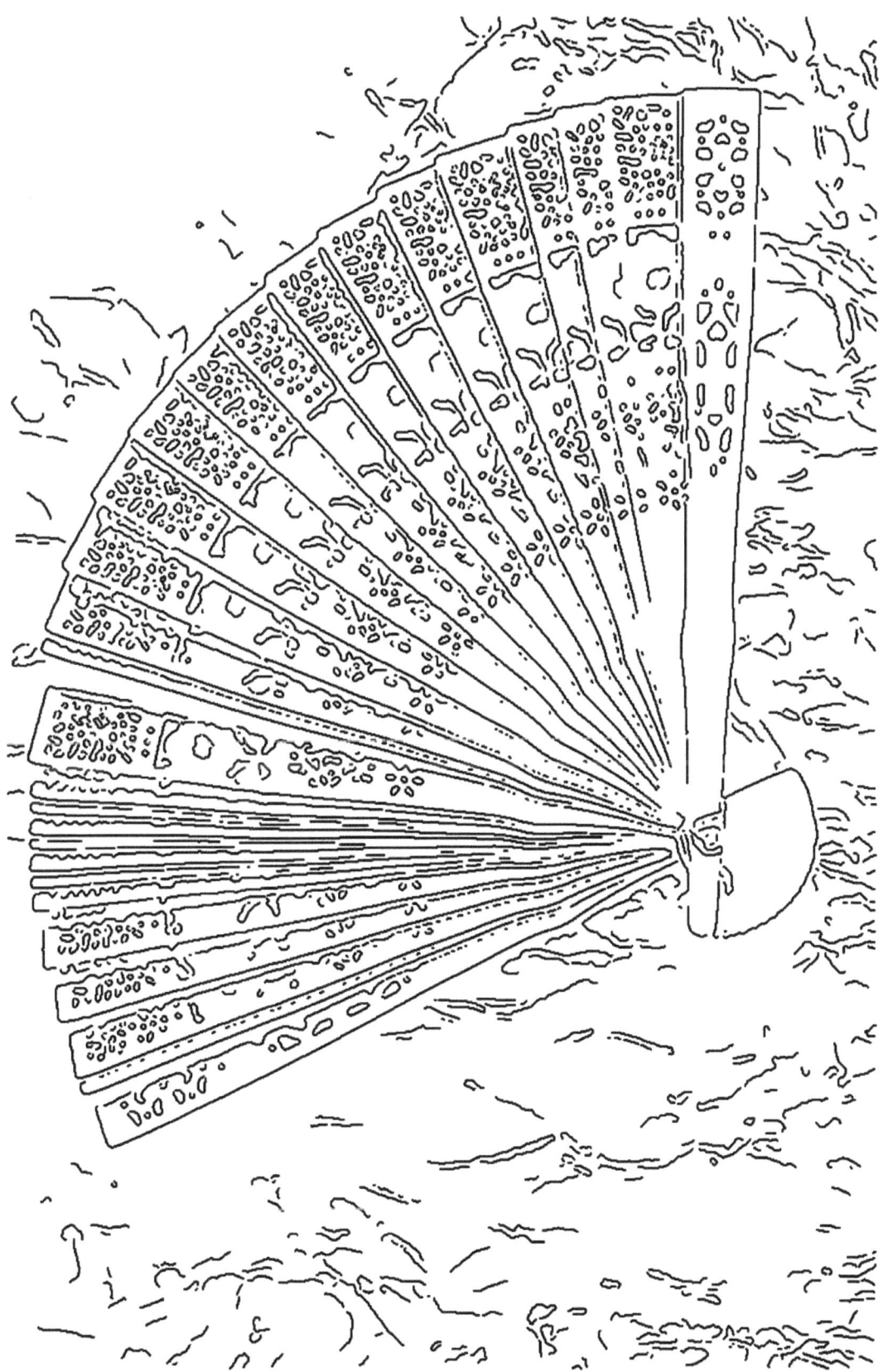

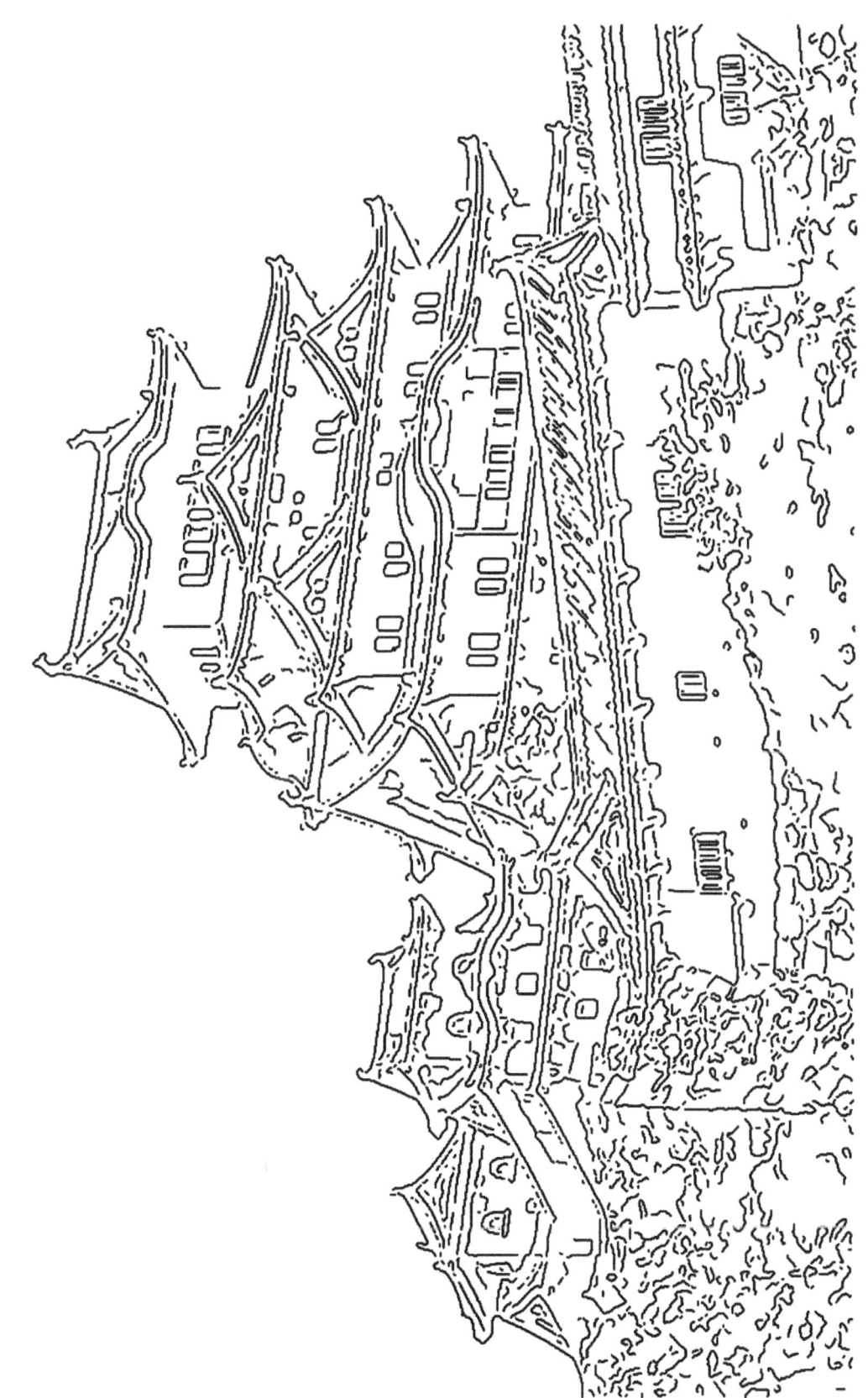

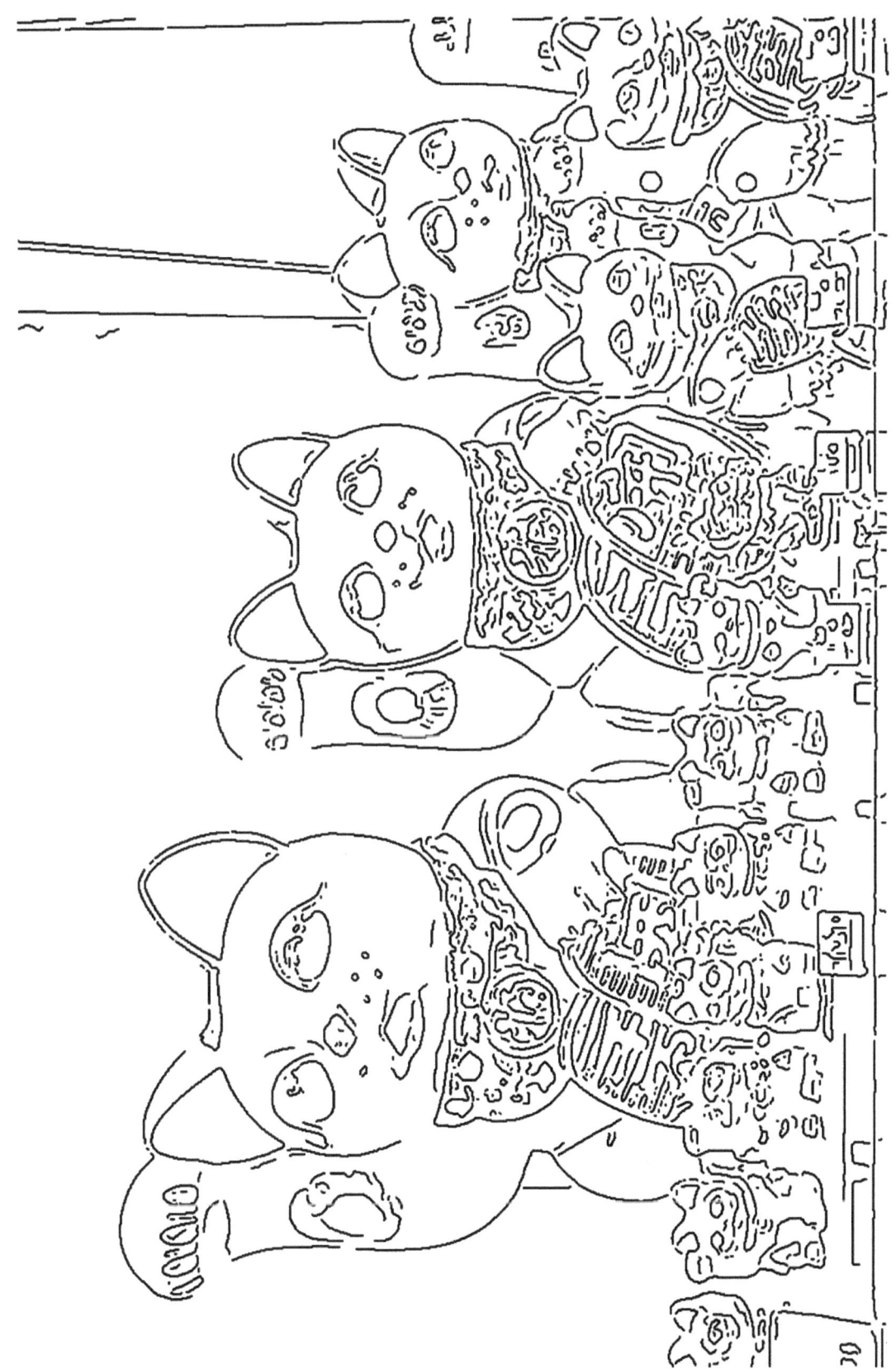

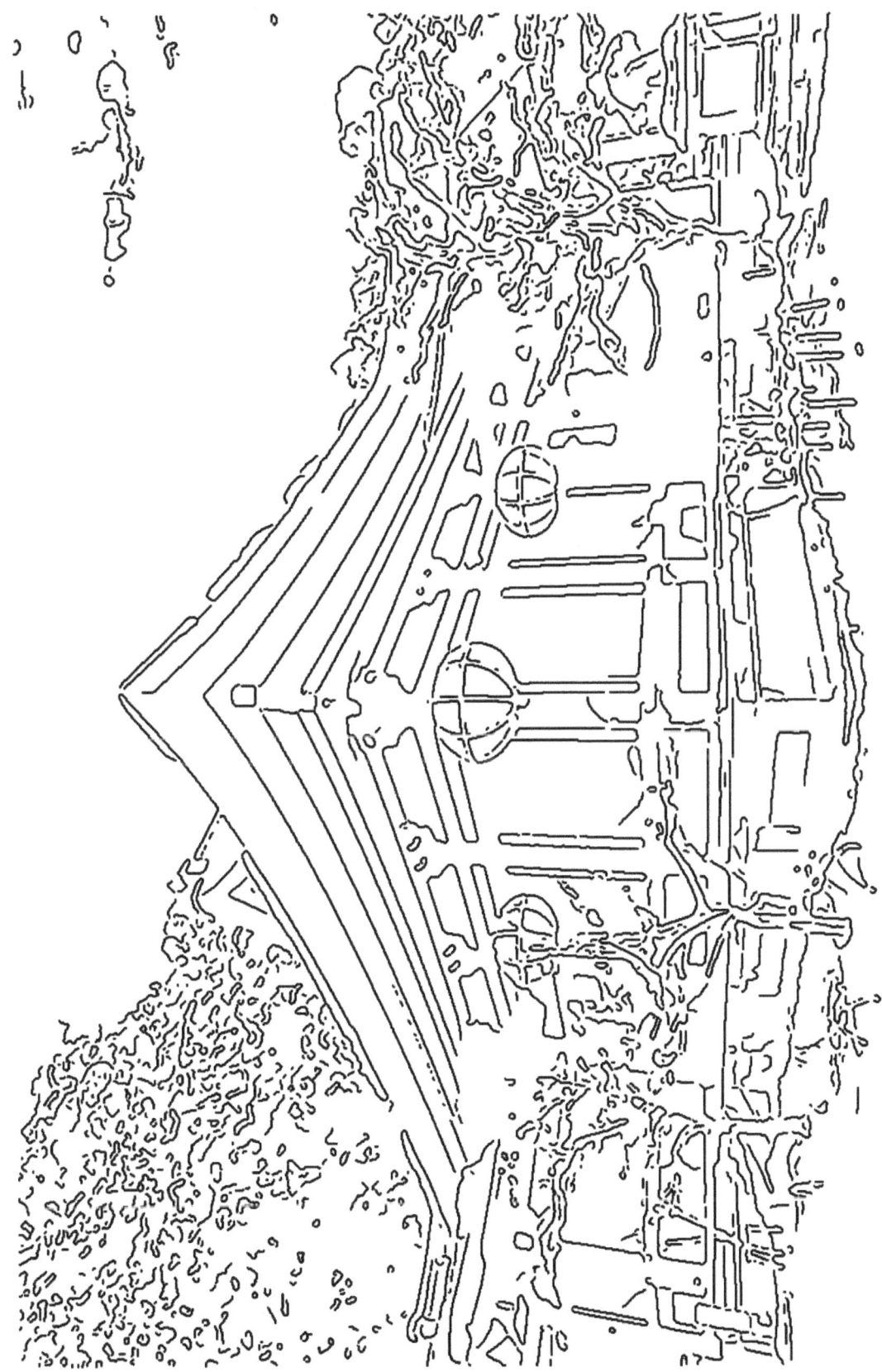

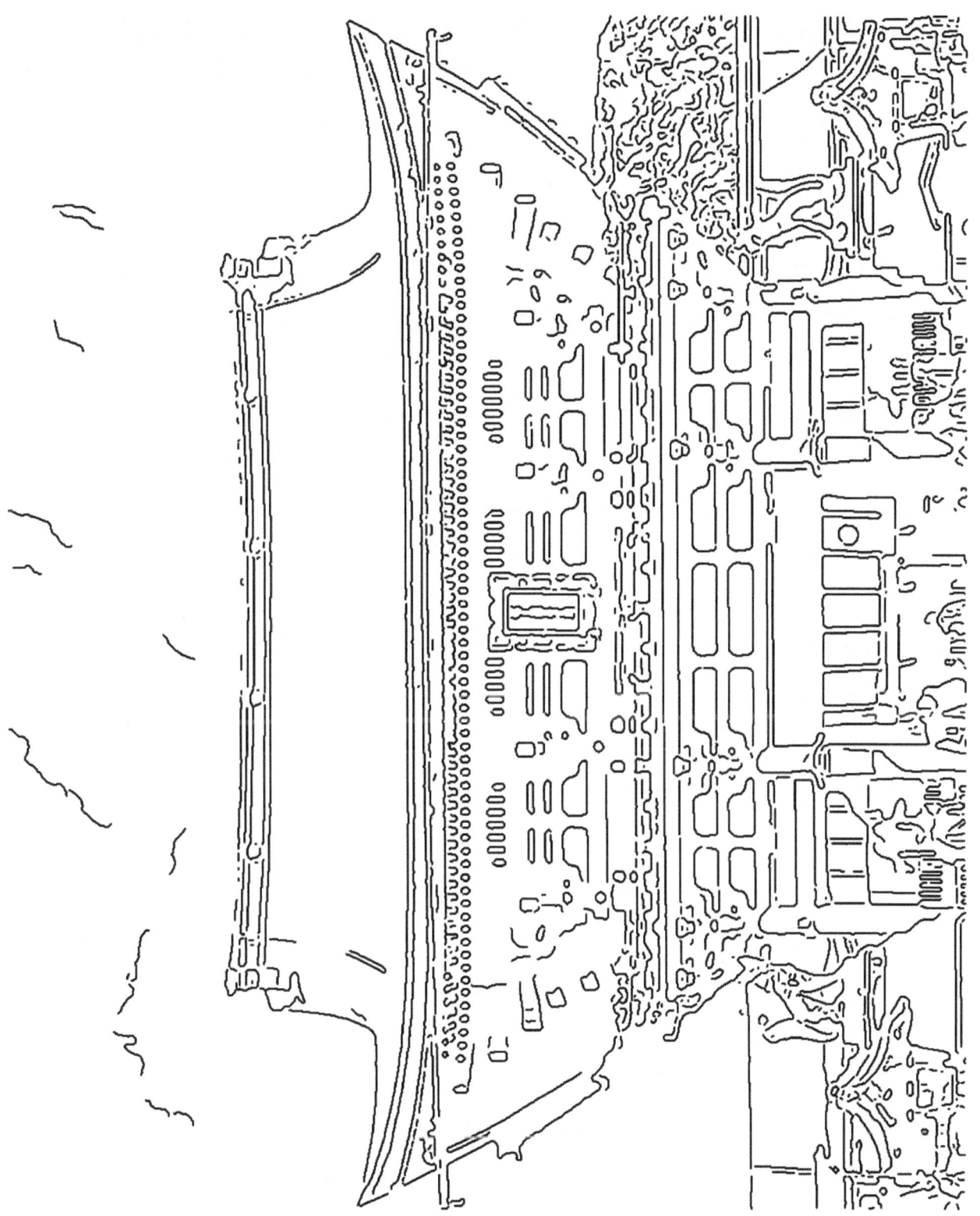

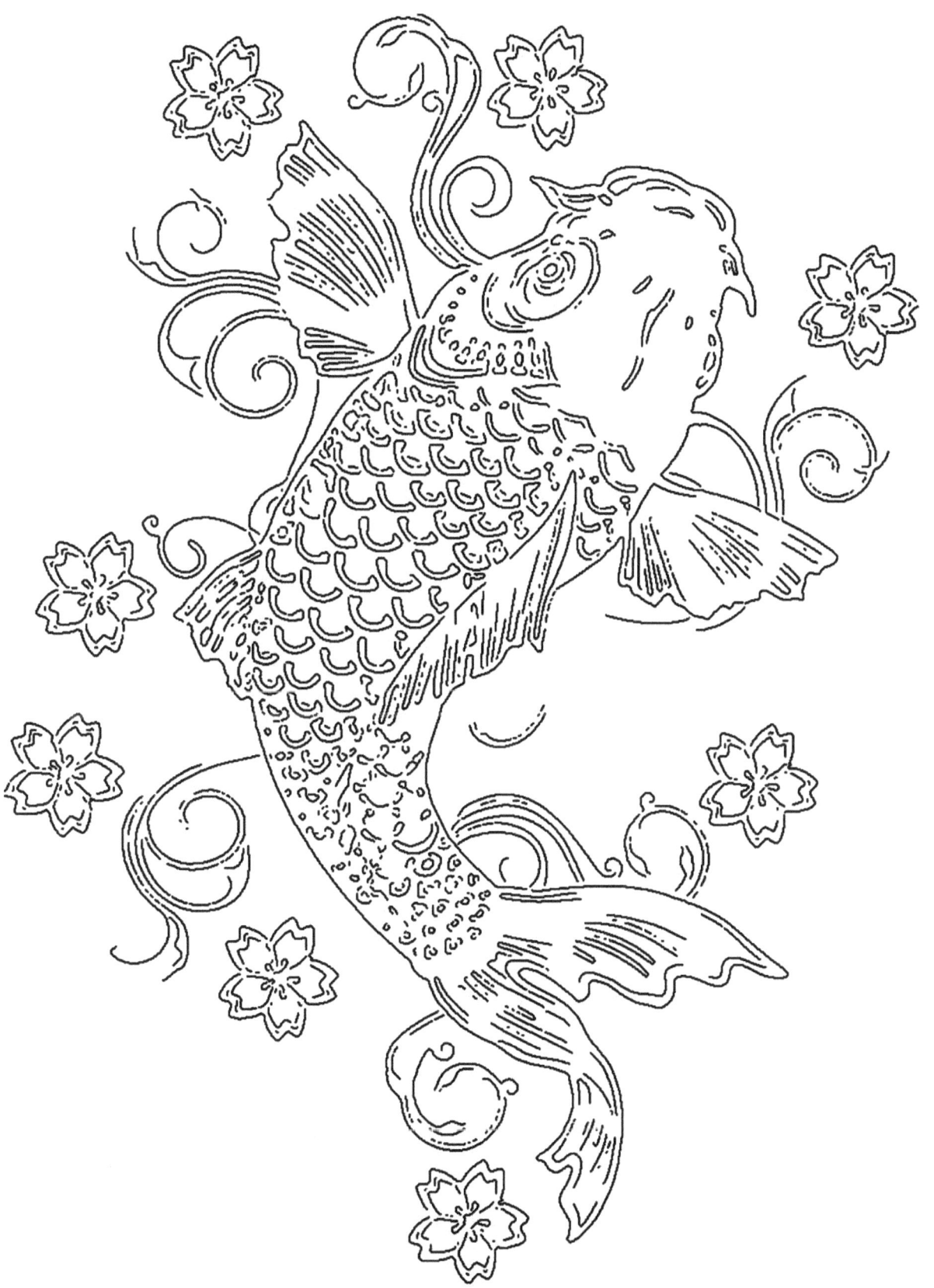

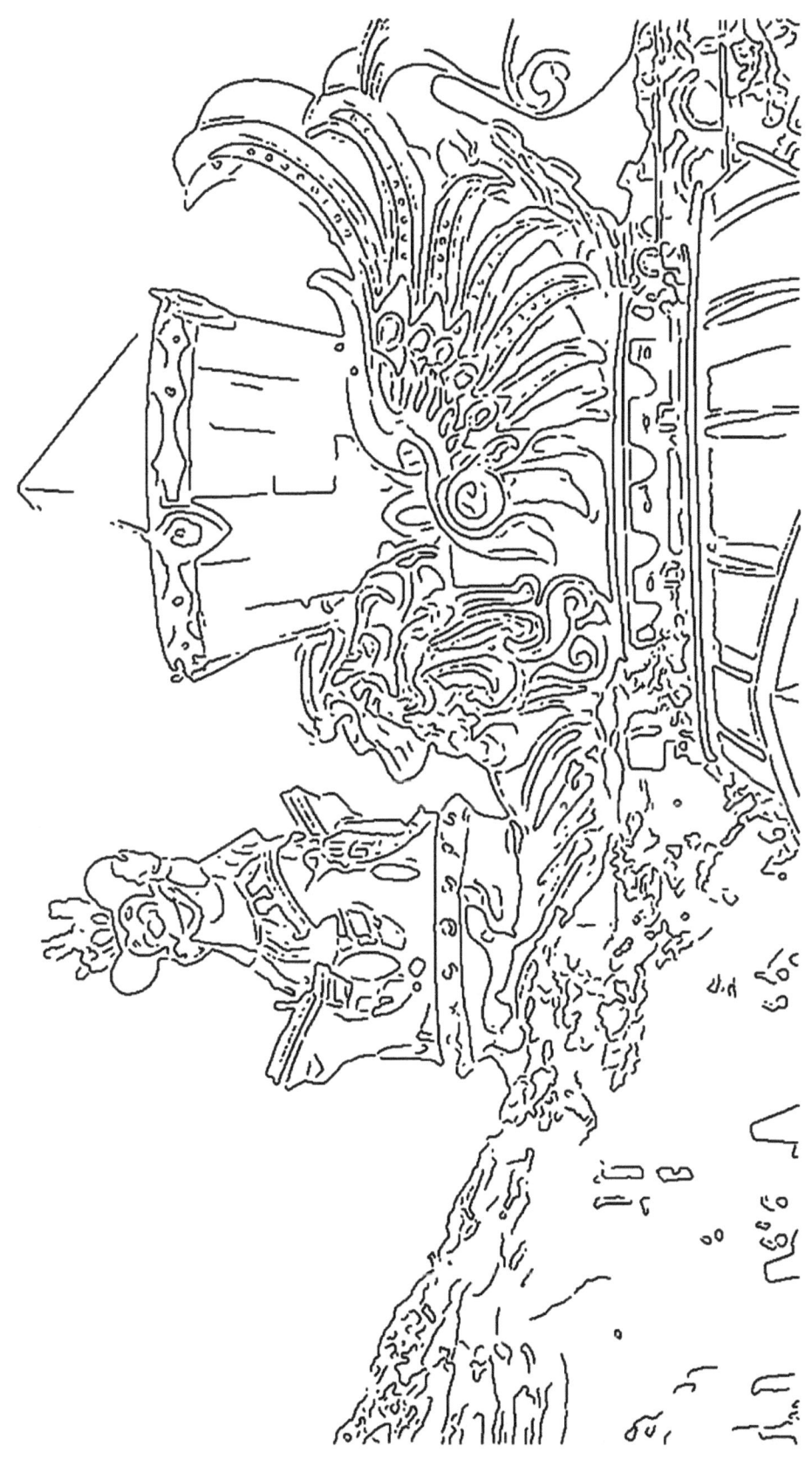

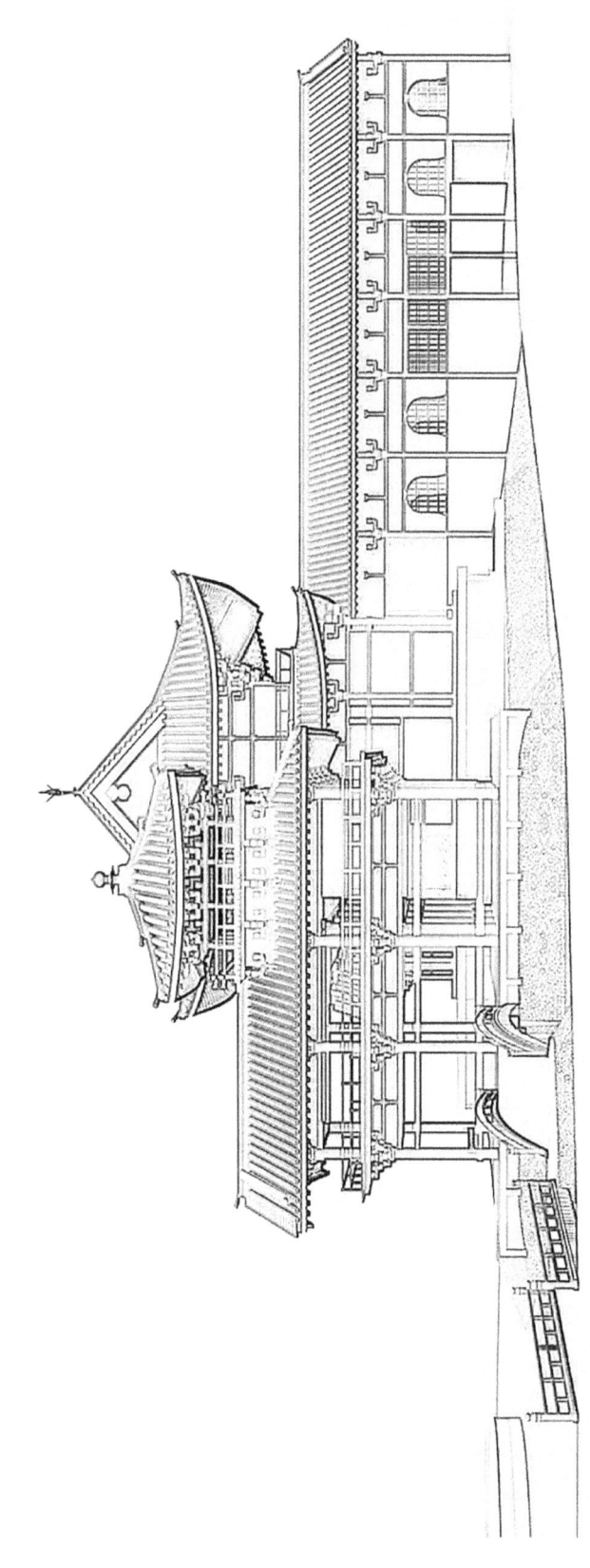

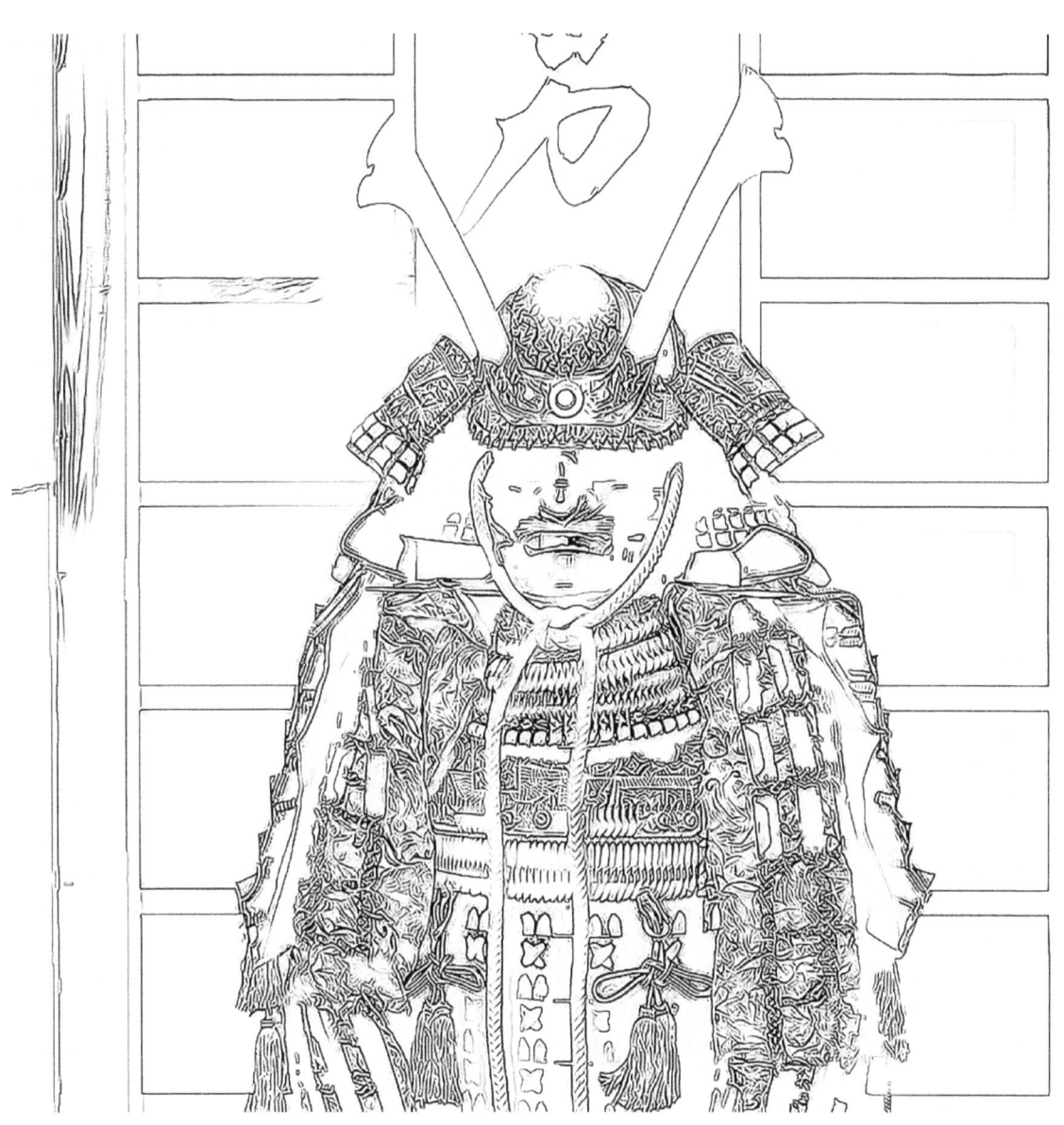

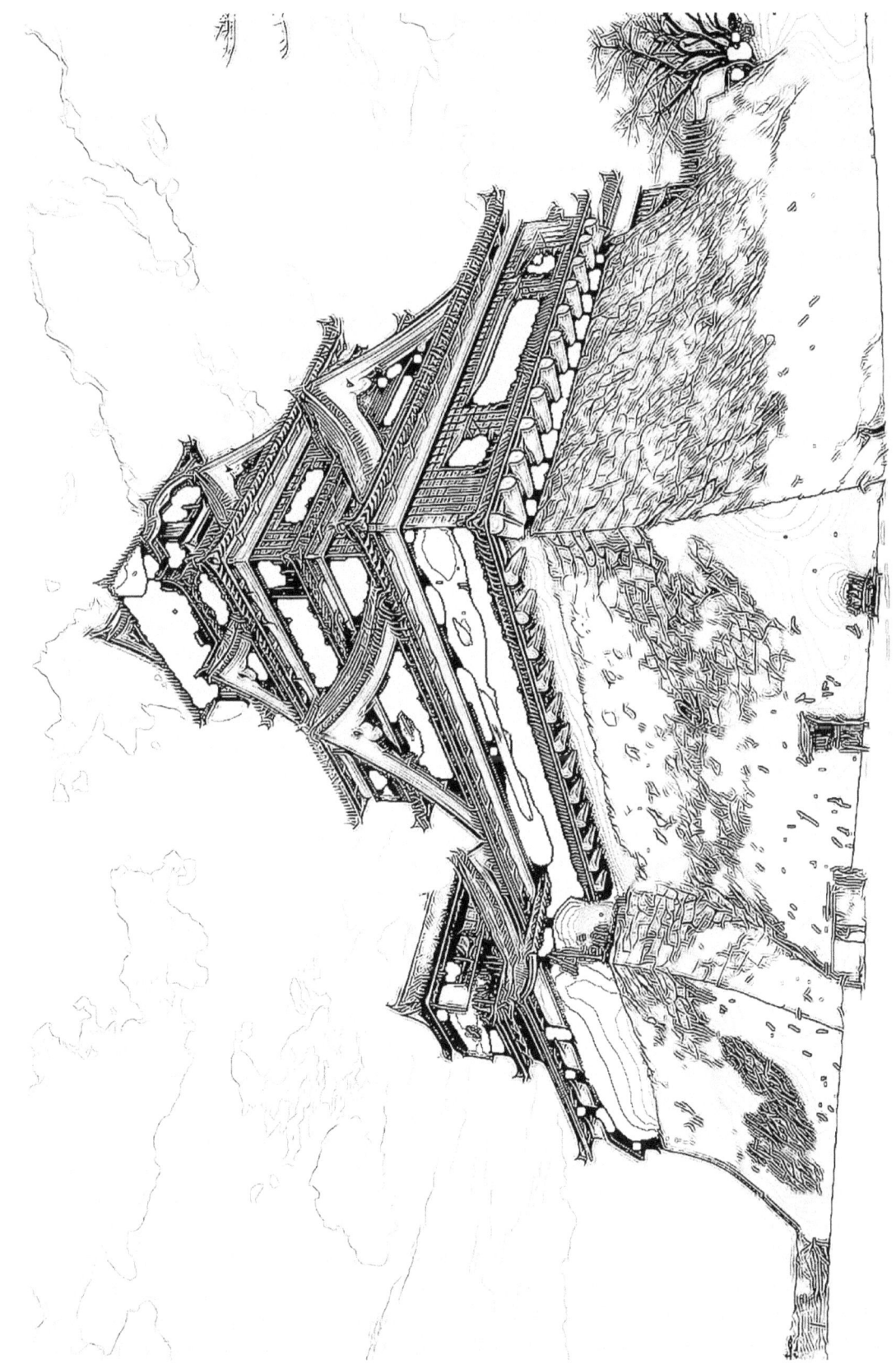

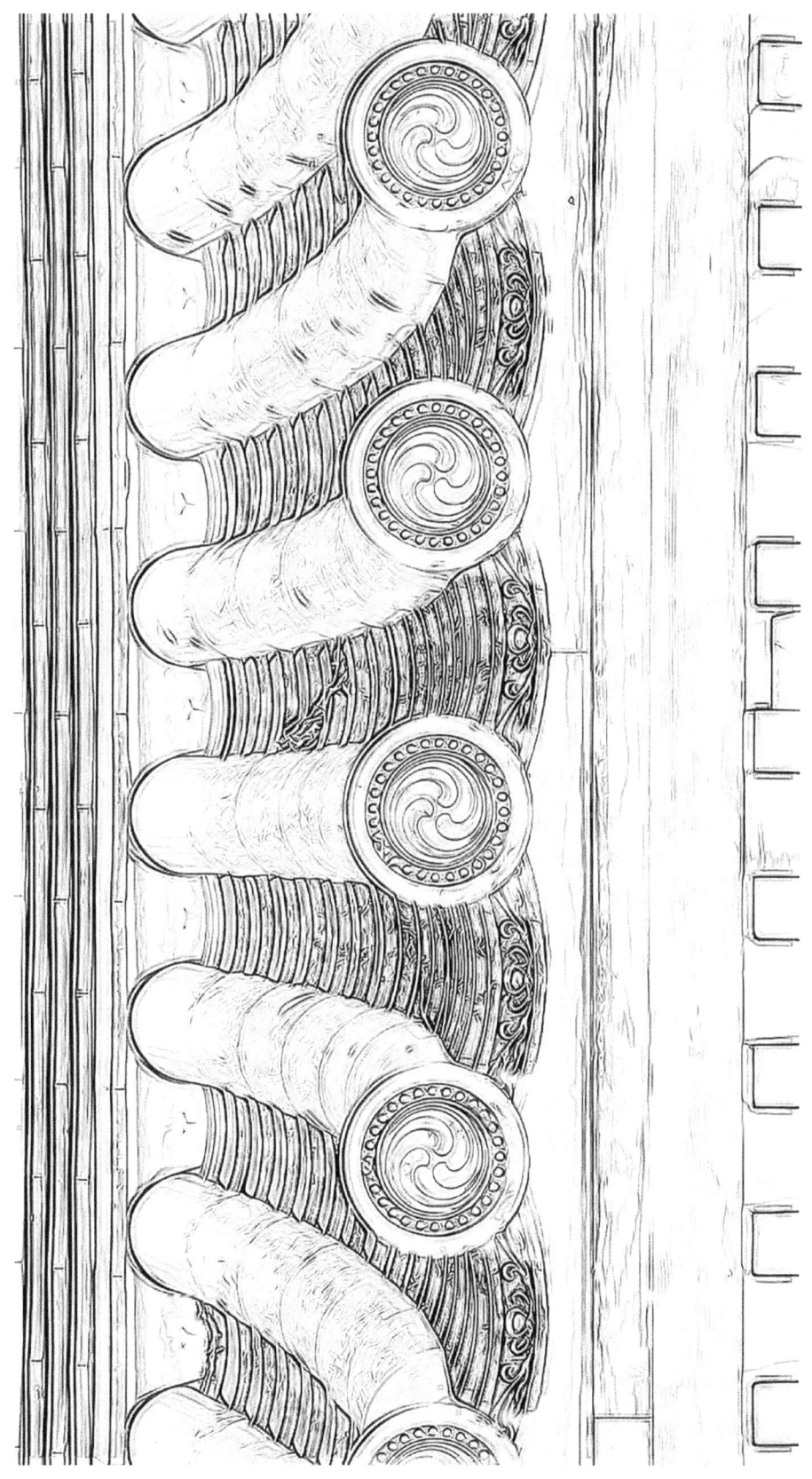

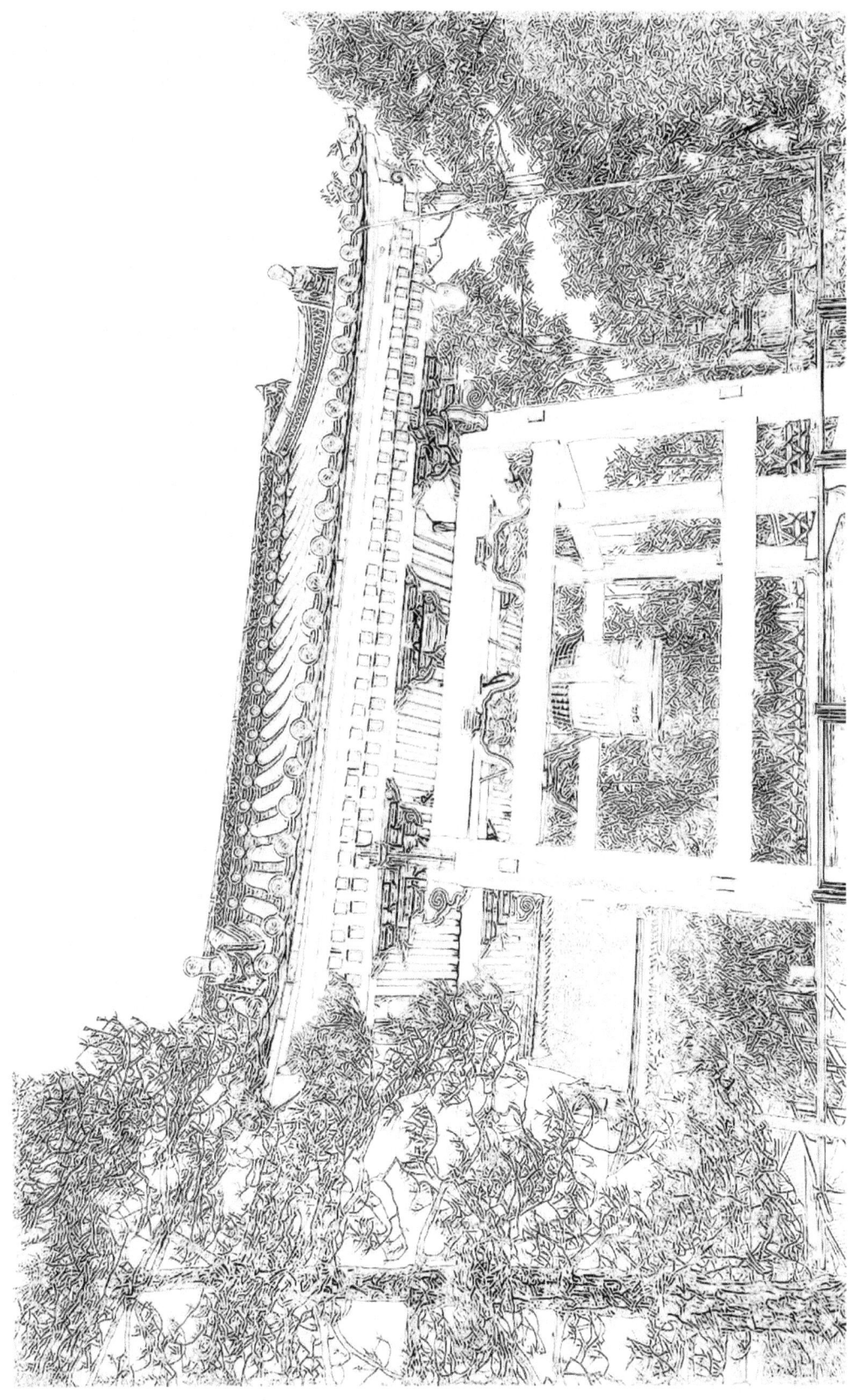

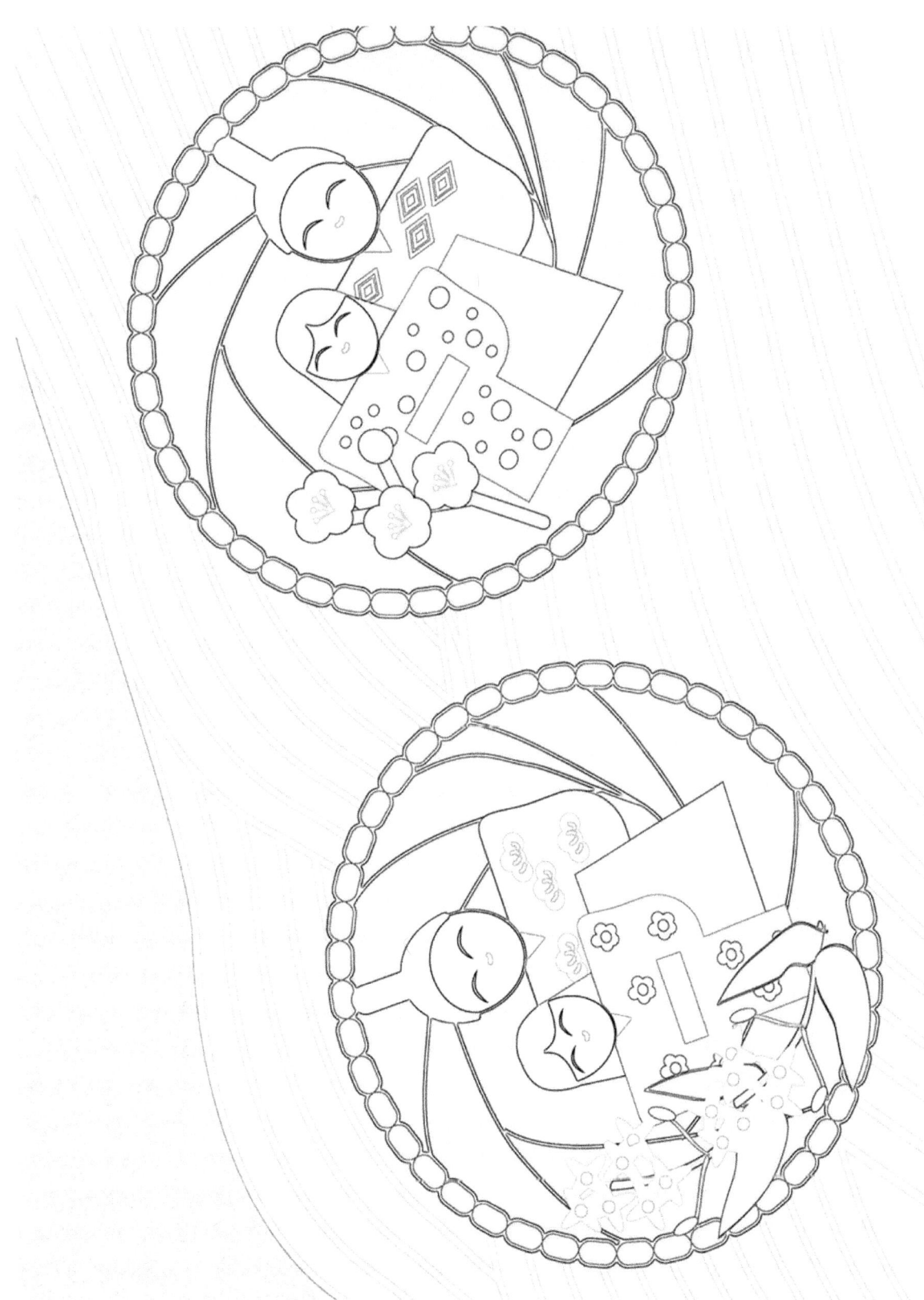

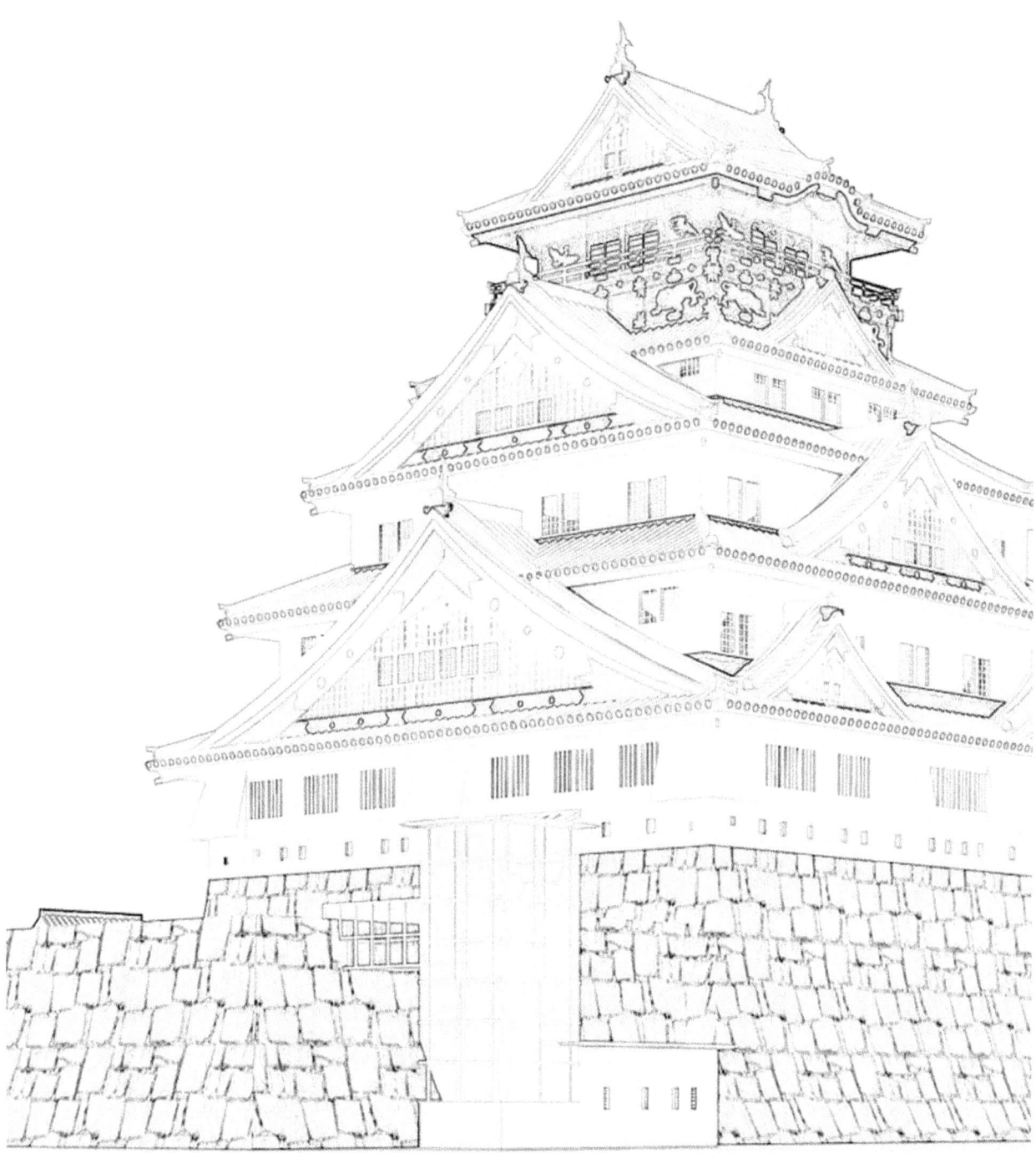

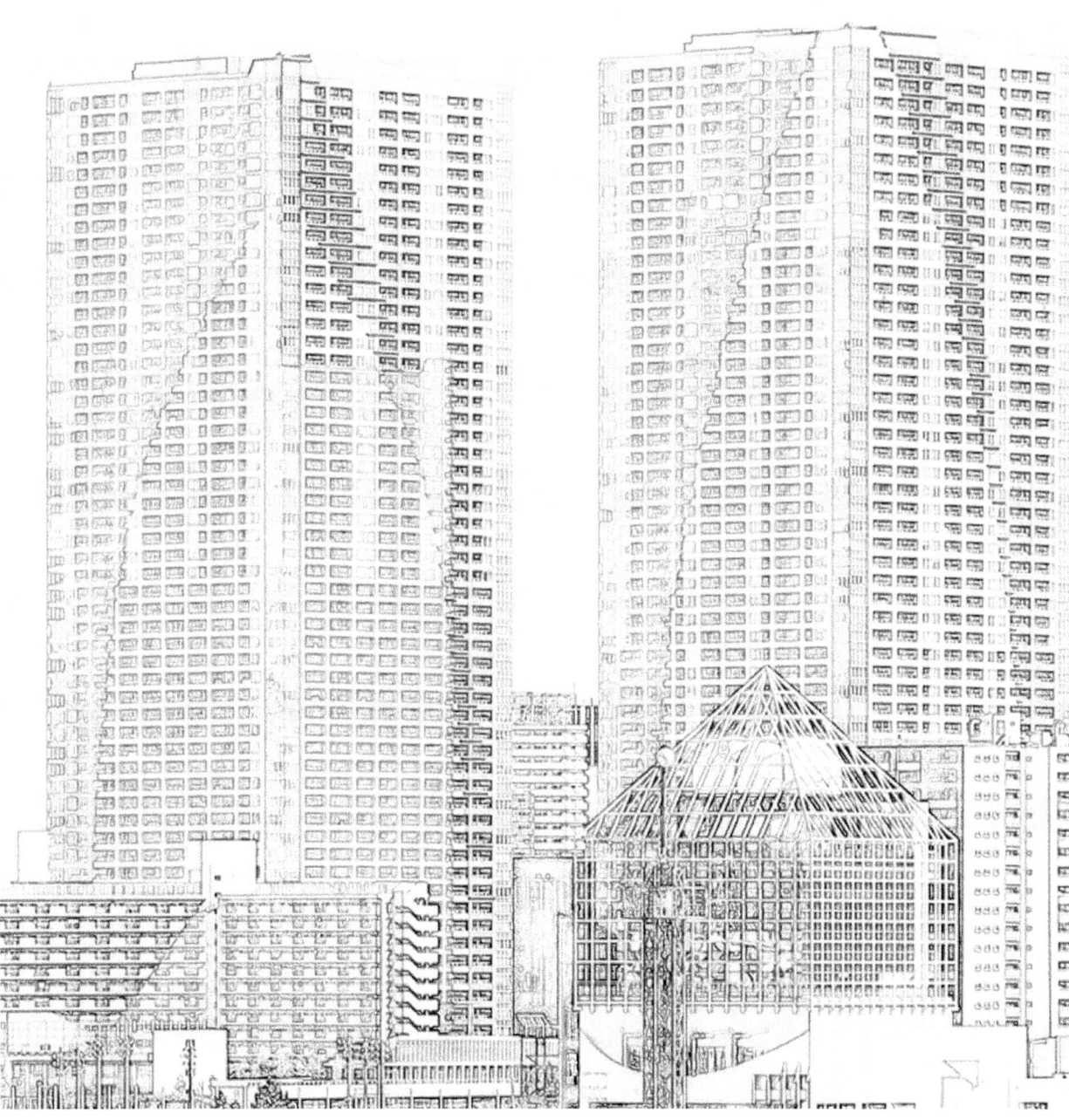

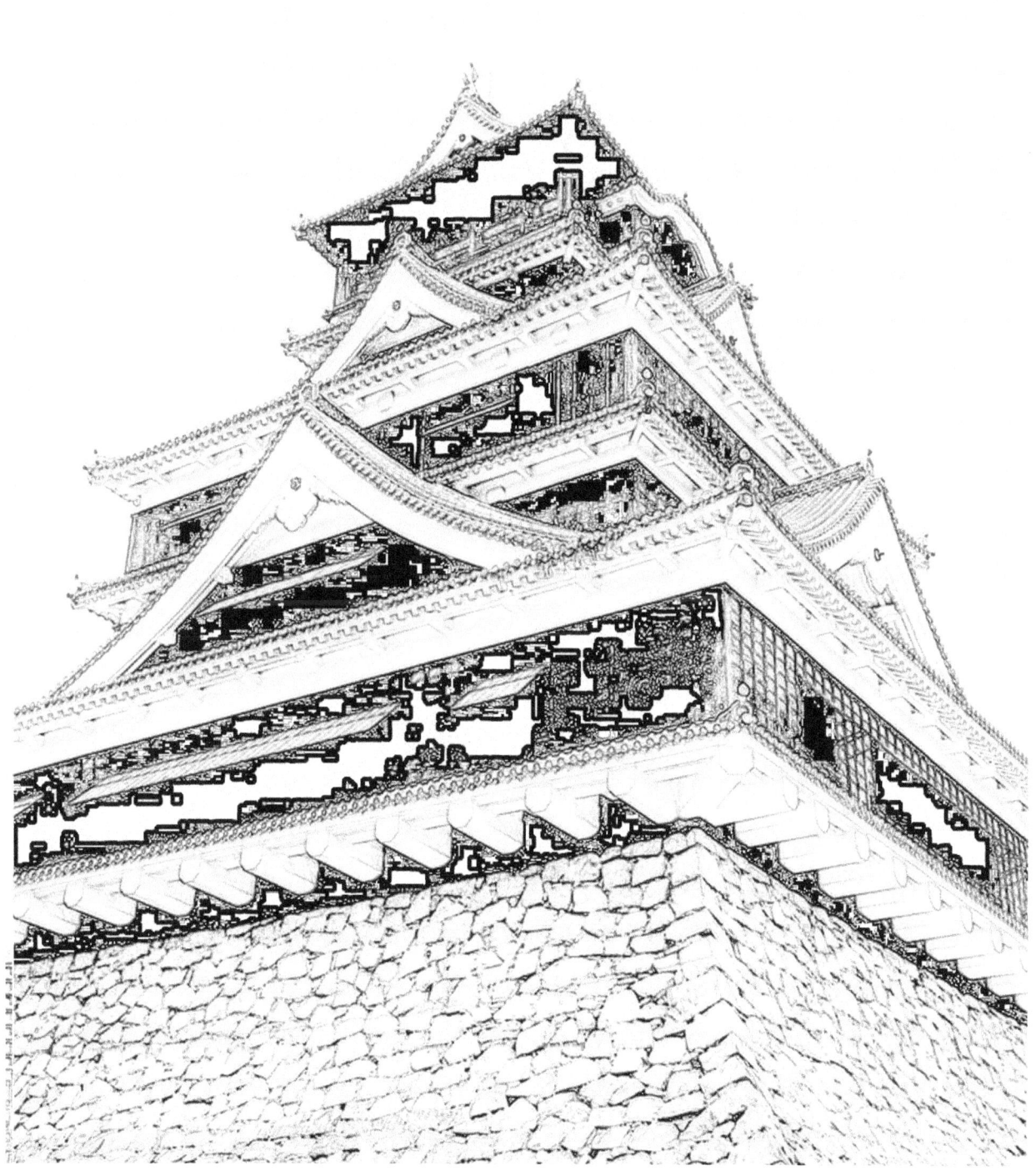

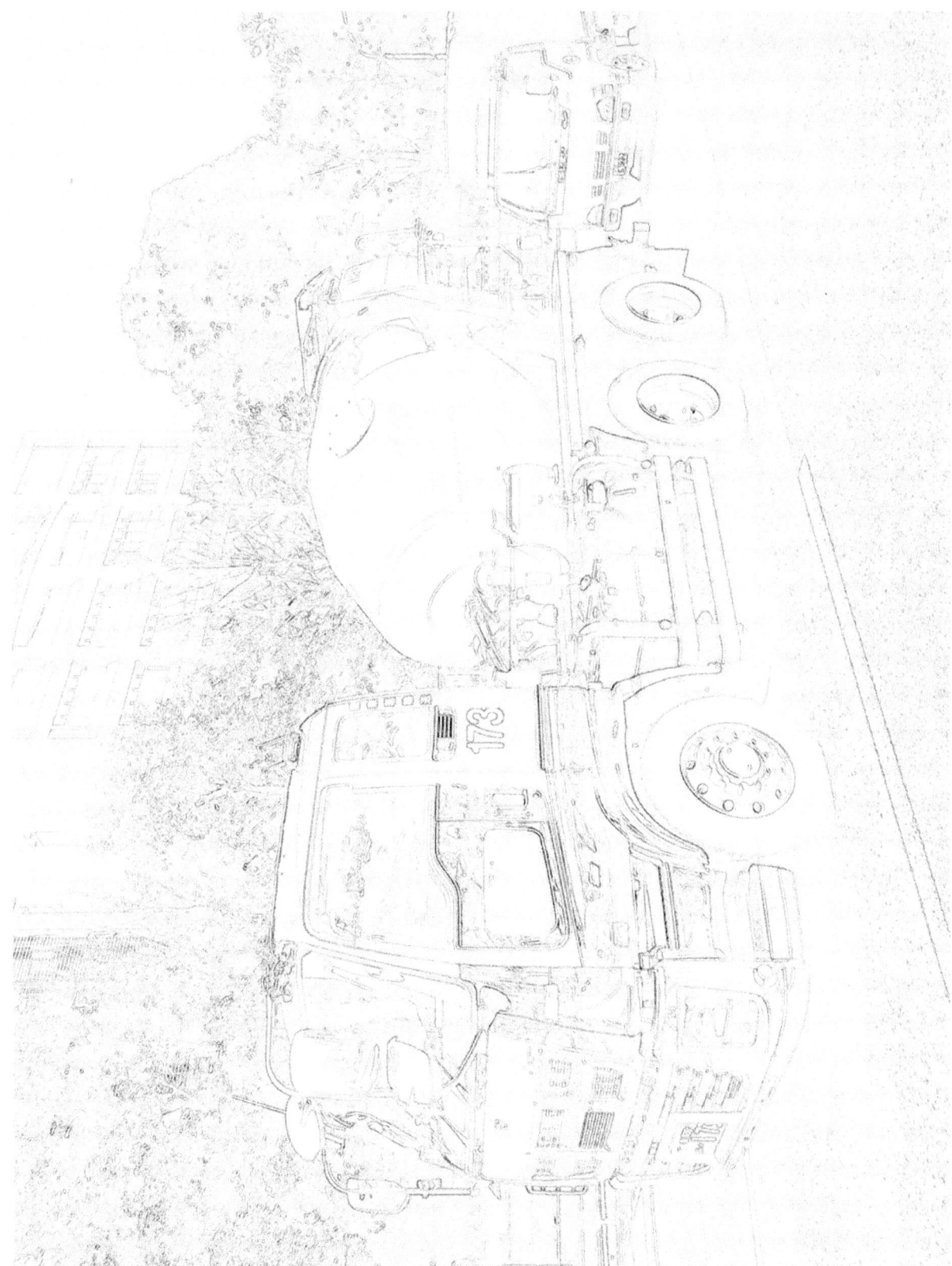

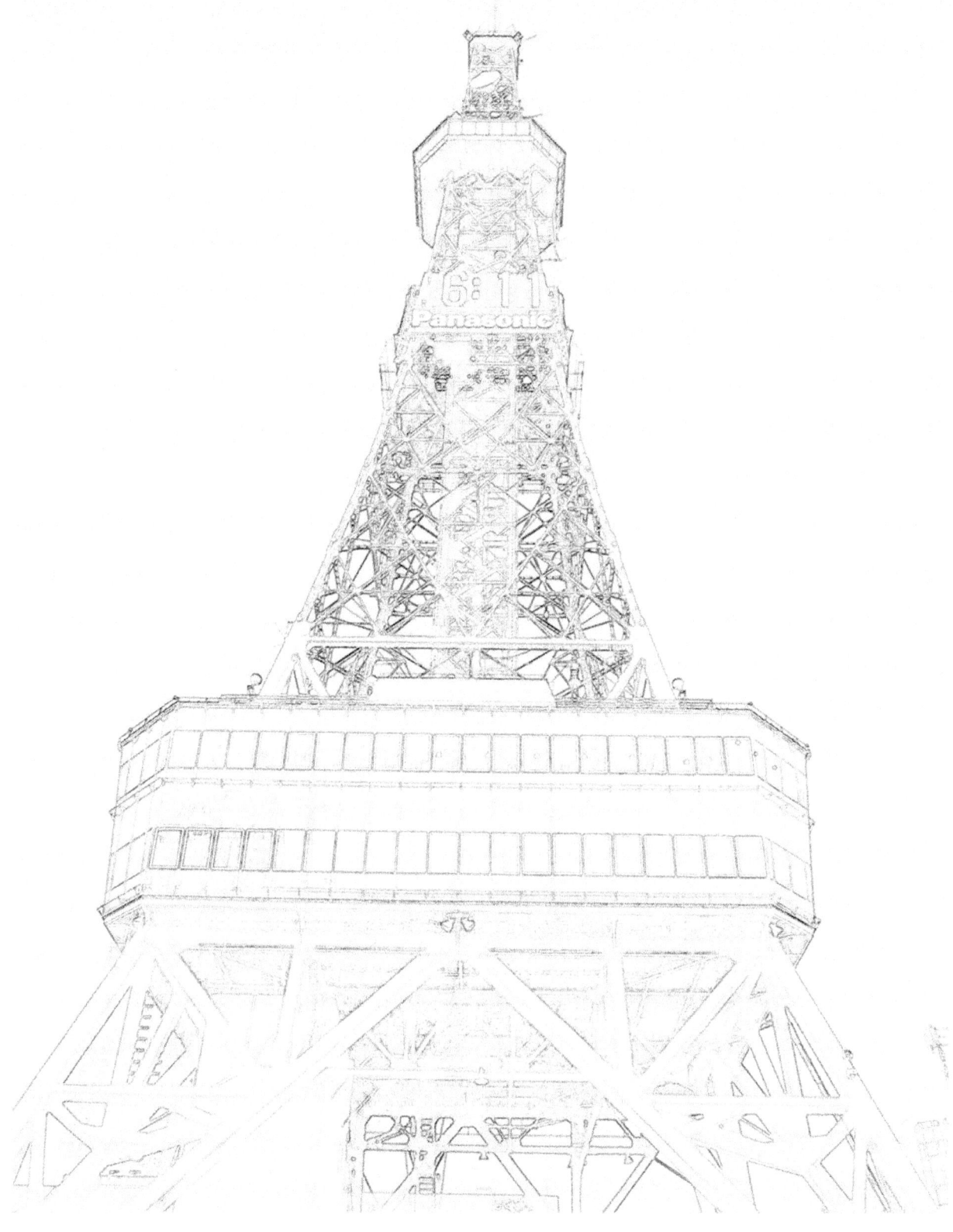

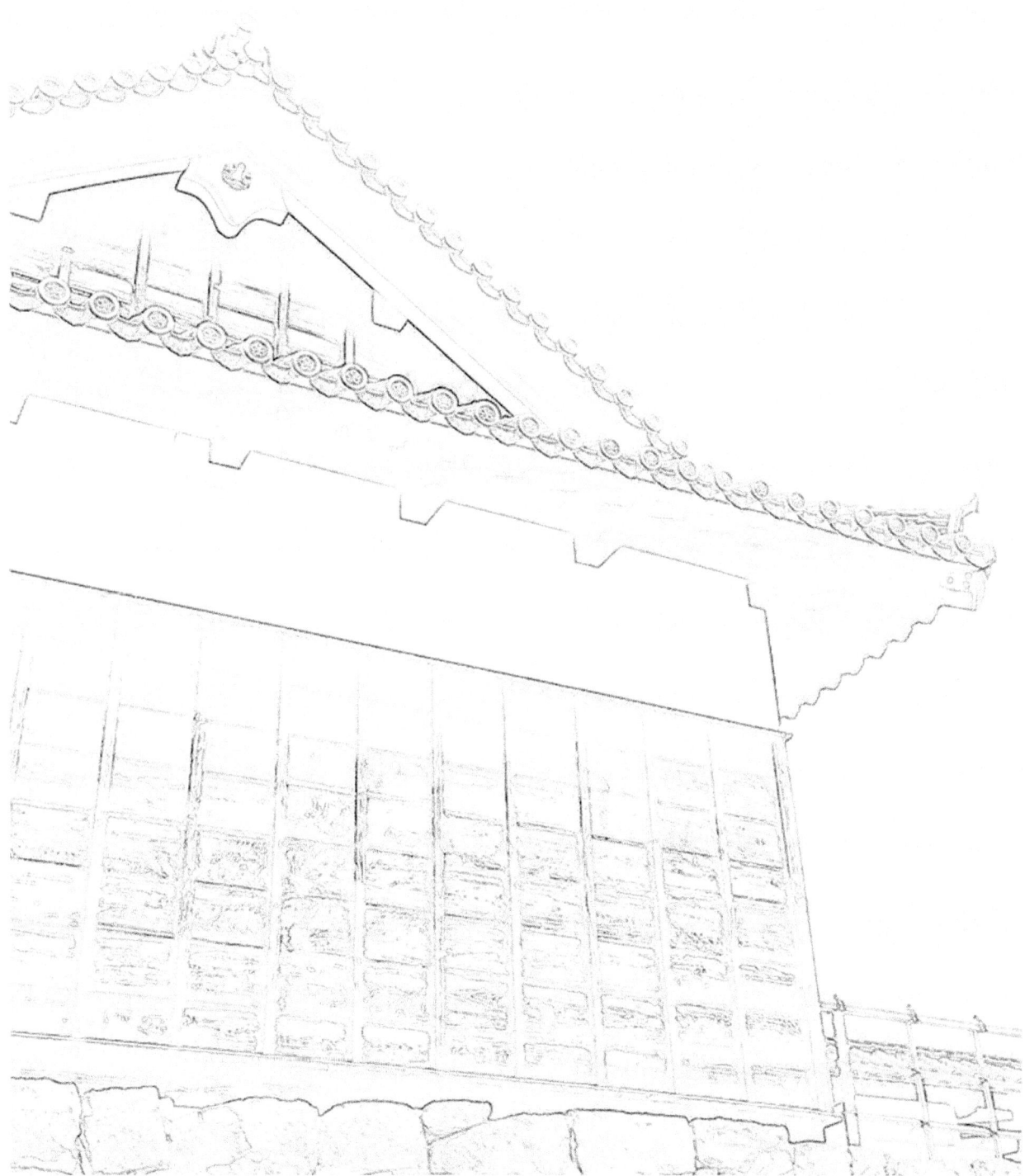

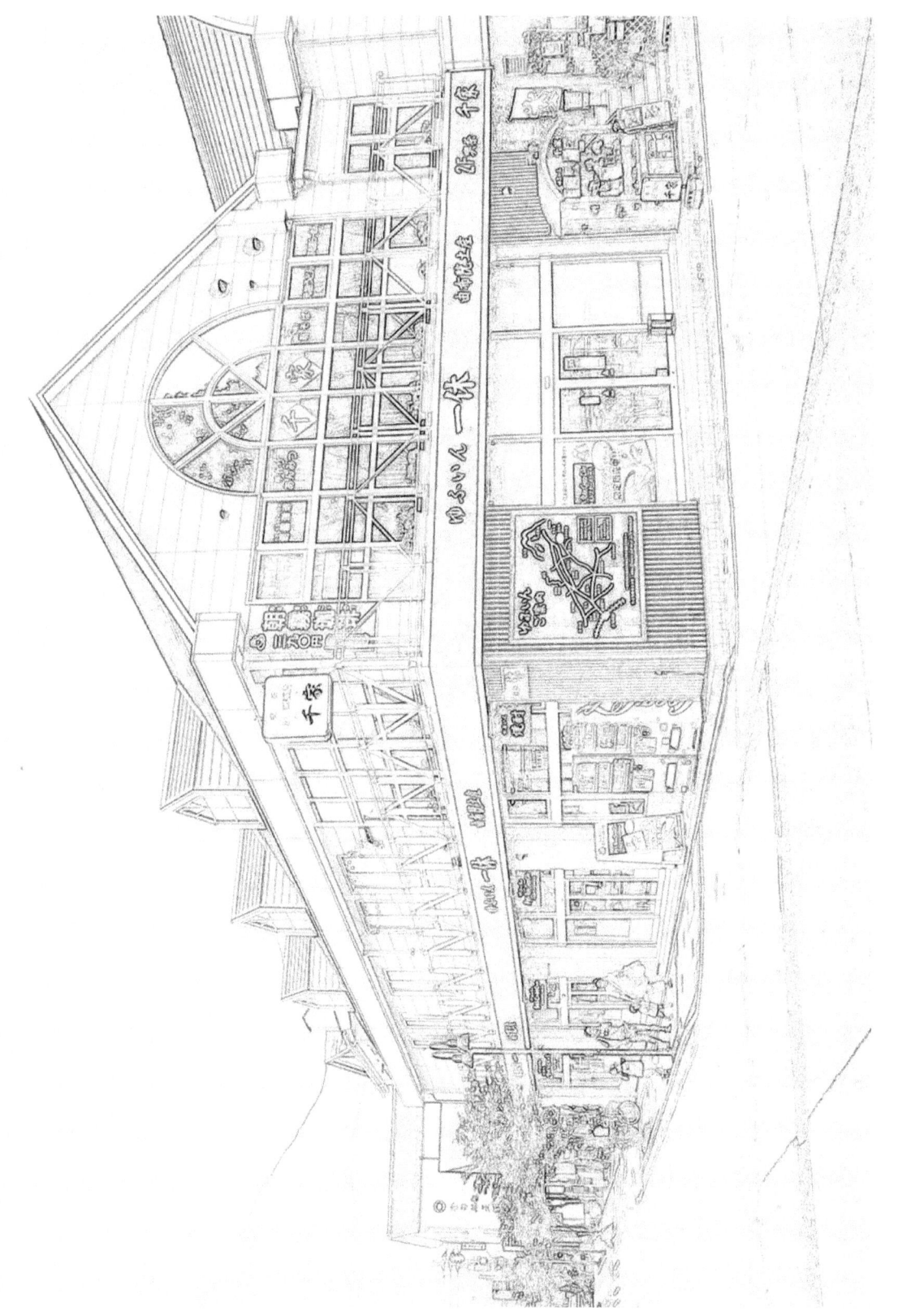

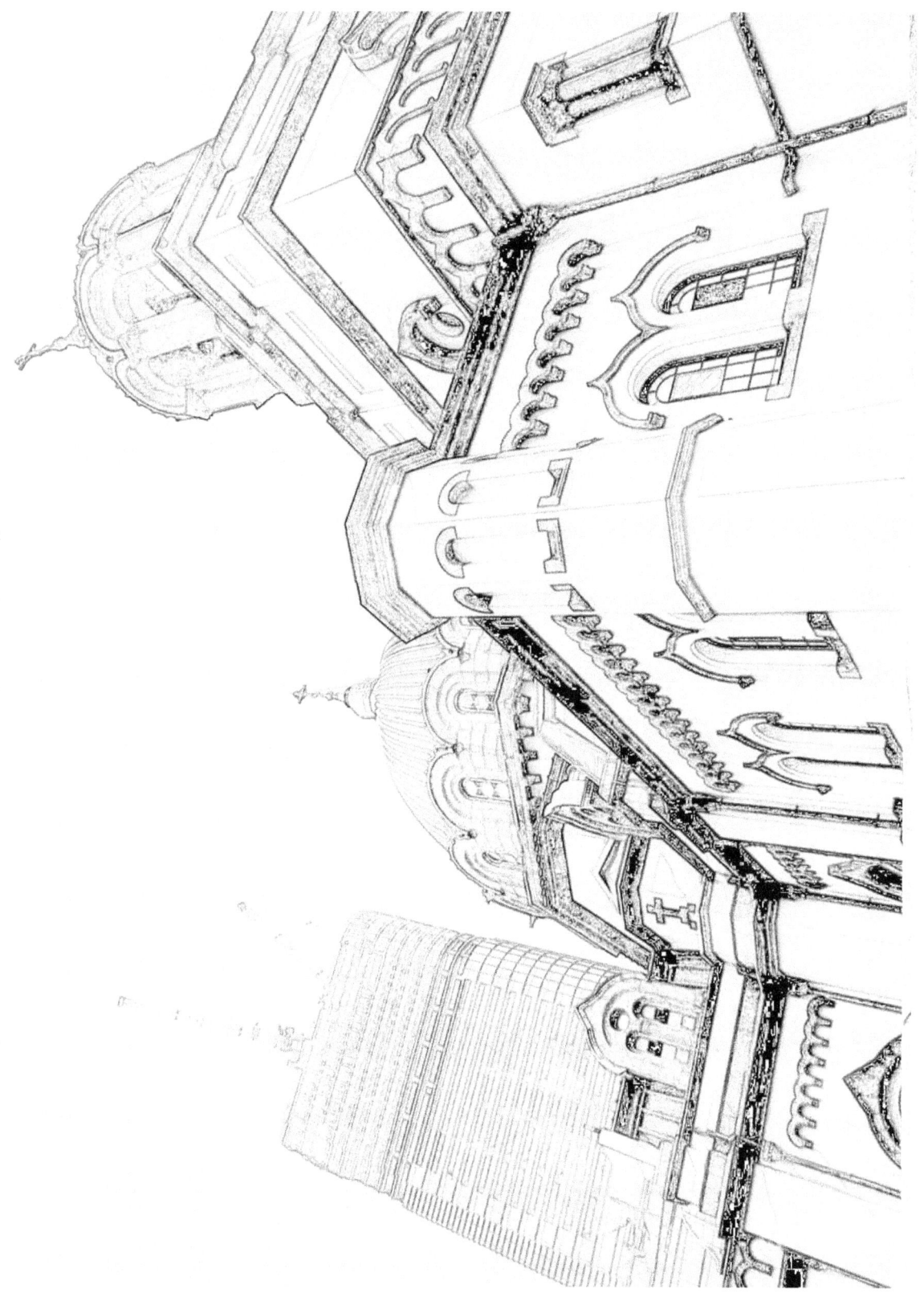

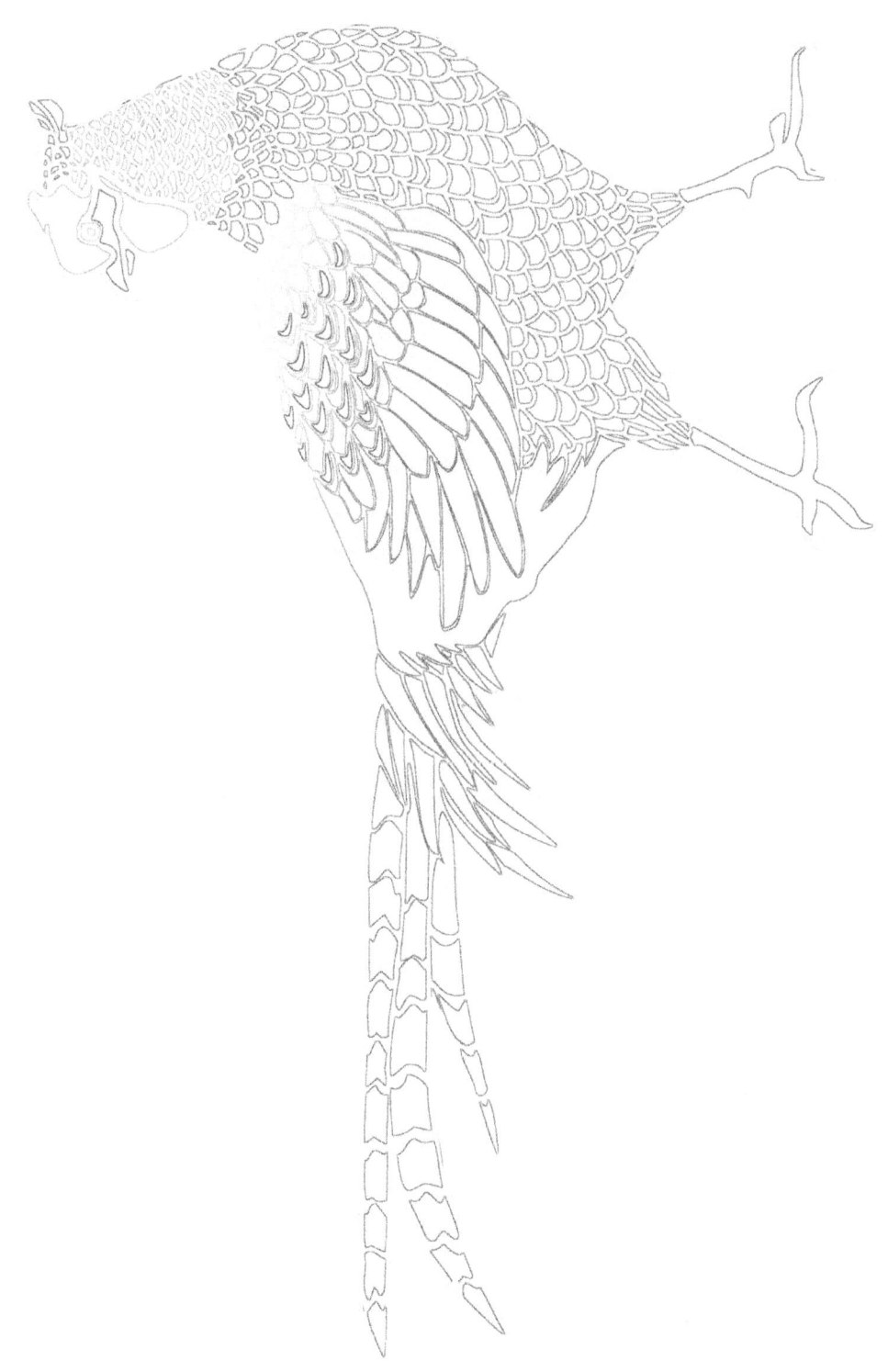

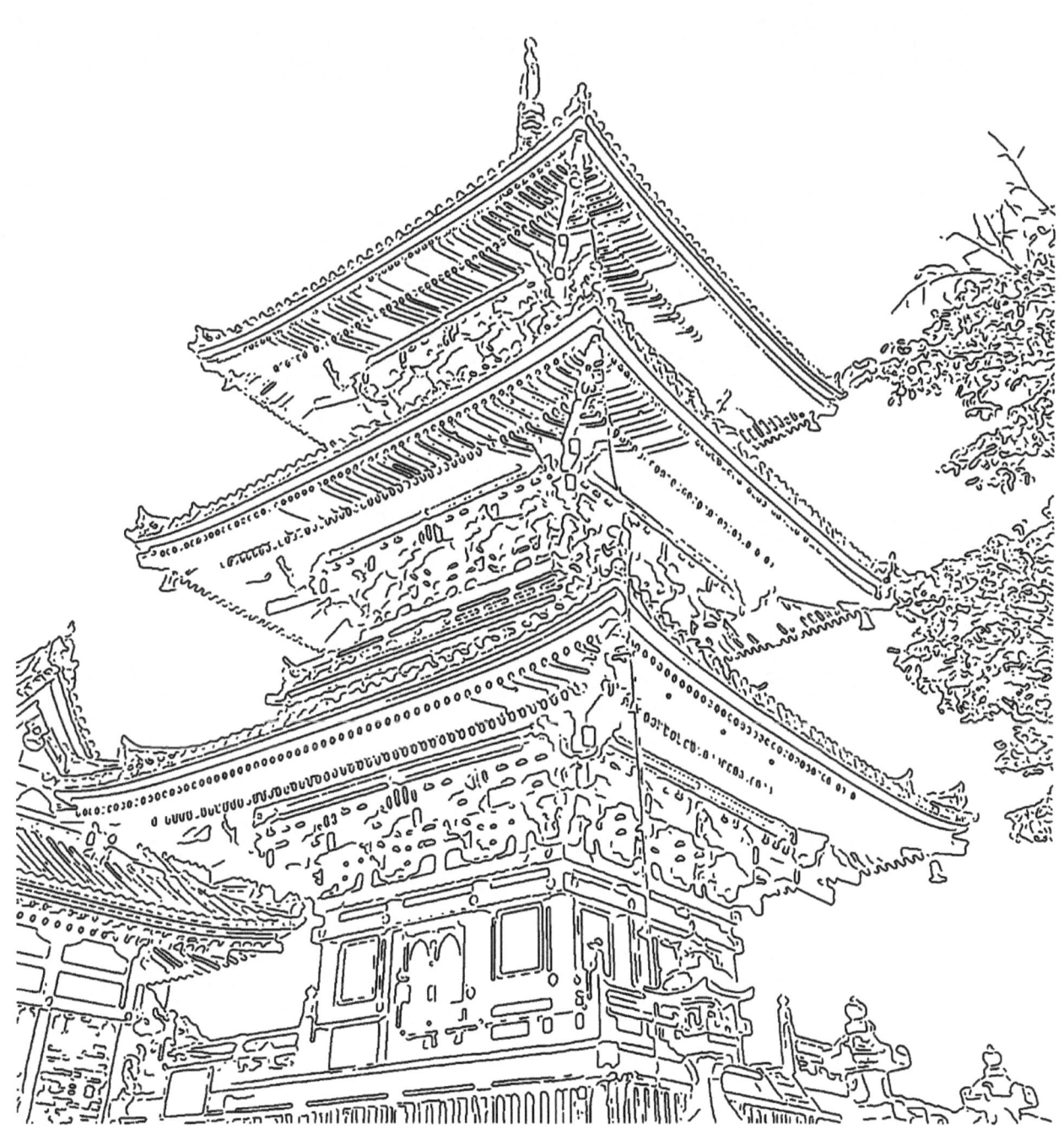

Thank you

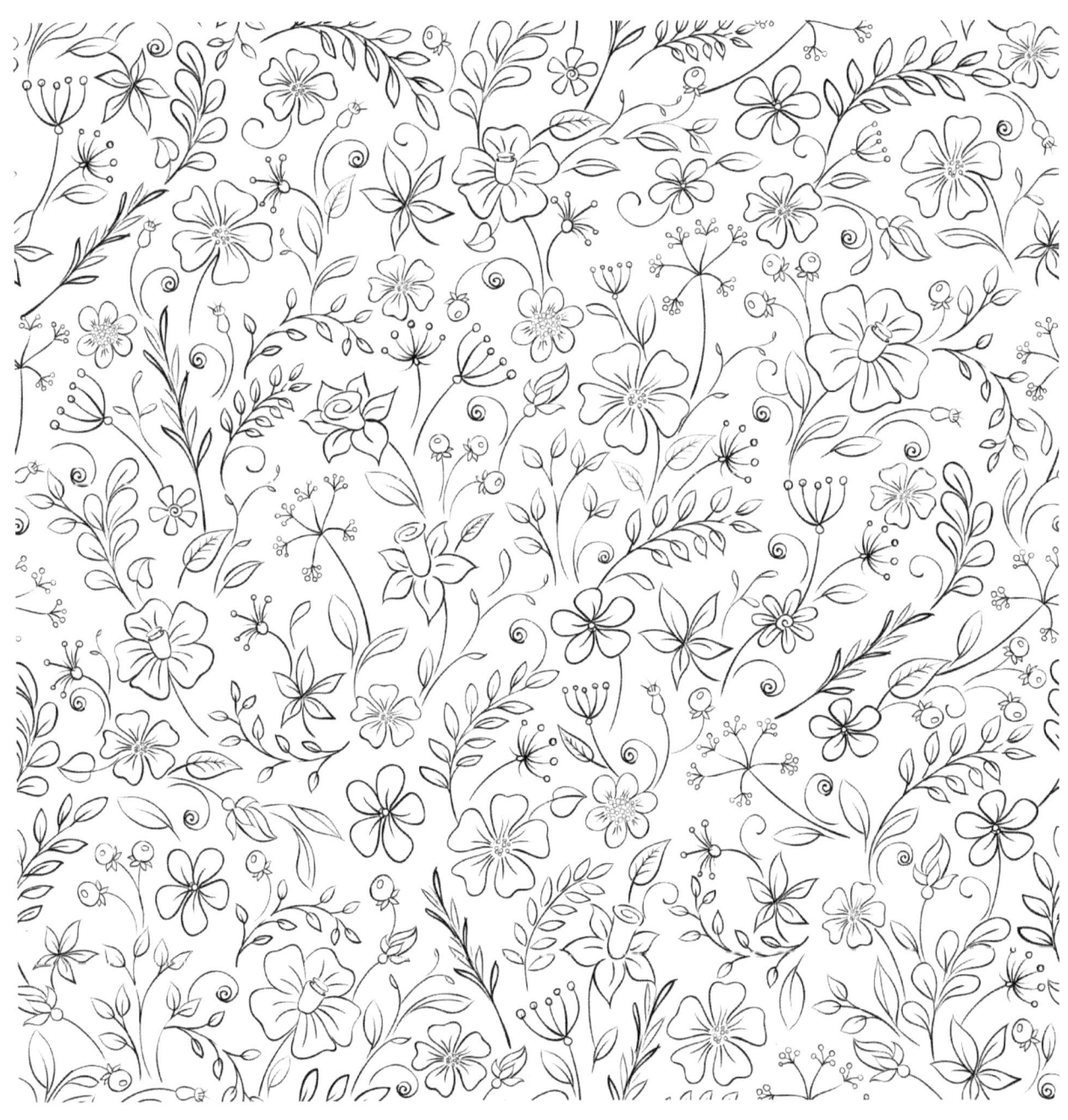

www.ingramcontent.com/pod-product-compliance
Lightning Source LLC
Chambersburg PA
CBHW080633190526
45169CB00009B/3377